I0493046

BR8K FREE
STRATEGIES
For Your Career

Acquire The Skills You Need To Market The New You!

RHONDA CHAPLIN

Love Clones Publishing
www.lcpublishing.net

Copyright © 2016 by Rhonda Chaplin. All rights reserved.
This book or any portion thereof may not be reproduced
or used in any manner whatsoever without the express
written permission of the publisher except for the use of
brief quotations in a book review.

Printed in the United States of America

First Printing, 2016

ISBN: 978-1534954458

Publishers:
Love Clones Publishing
Dallas, TX 75205
www.lcpublishing.net

ACKNOWLEDGEMENTS

I would like to express my gratitude to the many people who over the years have mentored, advised and worked with me through my own personal journey. I am thankful to God that He placed powerful and purposeful men and women in my life who were instrumental in utilizing their natural talents as an Employee, Entrepreneur, Investor, Ministry Leader or Foundational Builder to help me Dig In. Br8k Free. Br8k Out!™ Because of all those who have touched my life, I am now able to "Pay It Forward" and help others build and succeed in their career! I thank you from the bottom of my heart! I love and appreciate you all!

TABLE OF CONTENTS

Welcome! This book is written to not just give you an exciting read, although it will, but to give you a system to enhance and upgrade your career as an Employee! I know you and I have read lots of books over the years and we may question whether or not reading all these books have actually made any permanent changes to areas of our lives. Yet have no fear, this book will be different and it will make at least one permanent change in your life, but there is a condition. You will only see permanent change if you apply what you have read.

Throughout this book and within the pages of each chapter, you will find engaging exercises. These exercises are strategically placed for you to achieve the success I am confident you will experience. I want you to stop reading right now, yes, right now... go and get something to write with, so you can complete the exercises on each page. I want you to think of this not as an actual book, but more like your personal notebook or journal.

So, you may be asking, why did I write this personal notebook for you? Rev. Dr. Iyanla Vanzant said it best, "The greatest thing about teaching is that you can't teach it until you have learnt it and you haven't learnt it until your behavior has changed. It does not matter what you know—you can know a lot—but if it does not change who you are, then you have not learnt." So, I bring you the lessons I've learned after working and serving as an:

- **Employee** for over 20 plus years in corporate and non-profit organizations as a Human Resources Professional,
- **Entrepreneur,** Author, Founder, HR Business Consultant and Talent Coach for Free Day Strategies, LLC and Br8k Free Strategies, LLC,
- **Investor** with a diverse portfolio of real estate, stocks and market investments.

- **Ministry Servant Leader,** Founder and Visionary of Esther's Rising, Inc.

I bring the lessons I've learned, so others, including our future generations, will avoid the vicious cycle of not demonstrating the power that exists within to succeed in their career.

We were not meant to live paycheck to paycheck. We were not created to live beneath our means. We were not given talents to use in a career that we hate. So, I ask you, are you willing to do what it takes to unleash your power to succeed in your career? Do you have a strong desire to go to work every day loving every minute of what you do? Do you have a strong desire to leave a legacy that alters the finances that will be passed on for generations? Are you willing to let go of things that have not worked in the past and be coachable to relearn things that will move your life and career forward? If you've answered yes, then this book is for you!

The time has come for you to run your race FORWARD towards your purposeful career! Stop struggling to do the things you "must" do and start doing the things you love to do! The time is now for you to implement what I call **DIG IN. BR8K FREE. BR8K OUT.**™ which is covered in this book. In the three sections of this book, you will find the roadmap that I believe will help you unleash your power in your career like never before!

For those of you wondering why the word Break is not spelled out in the title. It's because we all know the meaning of the word Break; however adding the 8 represents a new beginning and a new order!

Are you ready to begin your journey? Are you ready for your new beginning?

Great—You are long overdue!

Let's go!

Introduction to our system

According to the Macmillan Dictionary the meanings of the above phrases are:

Dig In - to press hard into something; to prepare yourself for a difficult situation; to begin work with great determination

Break Free - to escape from an unpleasant situation or person that controls your life

Break Out - a violent or forceful break from a restraining condition or situation; a forcible escape

How do these meanings apply to you? Whether you have a full time or part time job or looking to transition to another career, you are working and serving others with all different types of personalities, work ethics, thoughts and issues. Therefore, you will need to press hard, be prepared and armed for anything that may come. You will need to be **Equipped** with your 'Why' and pertinent information from subject matter experts that will prepare you for what's coming. You will also need to uproot incorrect or outdated information you have been holding onto. This will be obtained by receiving ongoing **Training**, which includes coaching and mentorship programs to bring implementation to meet your strategic plan, goals, and objectives. Lastly, you will need to confidently and forcibly break away from your competitors and **Soar** to new heights armed with your Career Brand Message and Wealth Building Strategy to ultimately educate future generations.

Let's look at it this way. If I wanted to successfully lose weight and keep it off, I would first need to analyze why I want to lose weight (my purpose), work on a new plan to reeducate myself and work with experts to change the way that I eat and view food (my equipping), be coachable by following the information verbatim not adding or subtracting from it (my training), then I will be successful, and would be in a position to teach others (soaring)! The benefit of it all is that I will have a renewed sense of maintaining a healthy lifestyle, but I would have altered my genealogy and created a new legacy of being healthy, wealthy and wise (my greater 'why')! What started out with my desire to only lose weight, became bigger than me. This change of mindset, thinking bigger will come from following the system outlined in each section of **Dig In. Br8k Free. Br8k Out.**™ Let's Go!

SECTION 1

Dig In – Assessing Your Plan

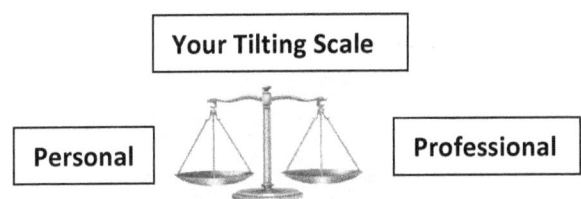

After reading this section, you will be able to:

- Establish a plan to bring balance to your tilting scale
- Identify if you are living purposefully
- Recognize areas of opportunity for personal growth and professional development

STRATEGY 1
BALANCING THE SCALE

Purposeful Living

Pur·pose·ful (adjective) is defined as having or manifesting purpose; determined; full of meaning; significant.

Purposeful living is when our lives have the most balanced and the most meaning from doing what we love for ourselves (Personal) and for others (Professional). Purposeful living is accomplished through BOTH monetary and non-monetary activities. Unfortunately, in our society we get too far off balance because we become so consumed by advancing our careers and making money that we neglect to spend any of our time doing things that bring us joy. Notice I said that bring us joy, not what brings our children joy, or our spouse joy, or our family joy but what bring us personal joy. We tend to give up our most precious, non-renewable asset that we have, our personal time to others (employer, client, family). Then our tilting scale leans heavily to the professional side and before we know it, we're frustrated and taking our frustration out on others at our jobs. We're depressed, angry and feel overwhelmed due to not having balance or an outlet. This can also work on the opposite side of the tilting scale. We can give so much attention to our personal life that we can get out of balance because we neglect giving time and focus to our professional side. In either scenario, the result is still the same. When the tilting scale is out of balance, we are no longer in a position to give effectively and efficiently to ourselves or to others.

This is why you must start here. Let's do a self-check!

YOUR TILTING SCALE

| Personal | | Professional |

IS IT BALANCED?

What personal hobbies, interests, or passion do you have?

_____

_____

_____

_____

How much time daily, weekly or monthly do you spend on your hobbies, interests, or passion?

_____

_____

_____

_____

How many hours do you spend at your or business per week? _____

How many hours per week do you spend lending your talent to volunteer work (this includes community organizations, church and/or ministry events)? _____

When you look at how many hours you spend working at your job or lending your talent to others in the community, in ministry, etc. does a minimum of 10% of your time weekly go towards your personal hobbies, interests or passion?   YES   NO

If your answer is YES, that is great, the remainder of this section can be used as an enhancement to what you are currently implementing and others will benefit from your story of how you maintain balance in your life.

If your answer is NO, like it was in my case, it's time to restore balance to your tilting scale personally and/or professionally.

Let's Go!

Benefits of Balancing the Scale

Are you stressed most of the time? Do you find yourself saying, "There is not enough time in the day?" Do you get less than the recommended eight hours of sleep most nights? How restful would you say your sleep is on a scale of 1 to 10 (10 being the most restless)?

For many years, my answers were, Yes, I am stressed most of the time; Yes, I wish there were more hours in the day; Yes, I get less than eight hours of sleep most nights, that's even if my mind and thoughts would slow down enough so I could experience a restful sleep for at least 3 hours!

And what was the end result? I would have to muster up the strength to go to work after drinking countless cups of coffee and as I arrived at the office, I hoped that everyone could see from the look on my face that I just could not be bothered, with anyone or anything! Does this sound familiar?

Being stressed, not getting ample rest, working all the time without having personal outlets is the most common reason for communication problems which results in conflict!

10% of conflicts are due to a difference of opinion

90% are due to wrong tone of voice

Another major obstacle of purposeful living is worry. You may find yourself worrying about this or worrying about that. It's time to get rid of being worried! Now, it's natural to be concerned about things. Yet there is a big difference between being worried and being concerned. If you are worried, it means you are seeing the problem, but if you are concerned, you will concentrate on finding the solution. I don't know about you, but I want more of my time to be focused on finding solutions! This is the primary reason that one of the values of Br8k Free Strategies is Resourceful. We believe that problems are opportunities in disguise!

Now that we have identified two major obstacles, stress and worry, let's look at the Benefits of Living Purposefully.

Focusing on Living Purposefully enables you to:

- Have less stress in your life
- Respond and react better to situations in your relationships, personally and/or professionally
- Focus on the solution and not the problem
- Incorporate your passions and hobbies into your life. So, whether you are single or married you will not be dependent on someone else for your total happiness and well-being.

Sounds like heaven doesn't it? Can you imagine working hard and loving what you do? Can you see yourself smiling for no reason? Can you fathom having so much joy in your life that it forces anyone having a bad day to just smile because you are such a pleasure to be around? Well, this can be you! Focusing on Purposeful Living can be summed up with these words, Live Stress & Worry FREE!

Restoring Balance to Personal & Work

In the previous two sections we outlined why we should live purposefully, how we can have it; when we balance doing what we love for ourselves (personally) and for others (professionally). We identified some obstacles, but more importantly we are able to see the benefits!

Now comes the hard part! Are you going to choose to restore balance to your tilting scale regardless of what some may think or say? Will you be committed to allocate time to invest in YOU? Before you answer, let's look at what balancing personal and work entails.

- **Time Management**
- **Planning**
- **Accountability Partners**

Time Management

When looking to balance your tilting scale, effective Time Management is crucial to:

1) Prevent increased stress levels

2) Create balance

3) Enhance productivity

4) Achieve personal & professional goals

By definition, time management is the act or process of planning and exercising conscious control over the amount of time spent on specific activities, especially to increase effectiveness, efficiency or productivity.

I have been facilitating Time Management workshops for over 10 years and I've noticed a growing trend. We are doing a great job scheduling appointments and meetings using the endless variety of tools and technology; but we're not using the same practice of utilizing resources to schedule the things we love to do for ourselves.

Planning

Failing to plan is planning to fail!

One of the great things about planning is that you can always change your plan, but only once you have one. Having a plan enables you to:

1. Set long-range goals and objectives linked to them

2. Establish priorities based on long term importance and short range urgency

3. Sketch an ideal day based on your personal energy cycle and best working times

Overall, planning enables you to put structure and order into your day, week and month. In essence, planning Puts You in Control; however the most important tip I can share on planning is once you have Your Plan you must have laser like focus to Work Your Plan! This is why I strongly encourage you to share your plan with someone that will encourage you to stick to it, someone that will not pull you away from your goal of balancing your scale, and who will be a cheerleader for you as you discover areas in your personal and professional life that bring you joy! This person would also be known as your Accountability Partner.

Accountability Partner

What is an accountability partner?

An accountability partner takes on the role as a trusted confident who you can trust and who can provide you with the guidance and motivation to forge ahead along your journey. They will help you keep committed and totally responsible for your actions and behaviors in reaching your goals. Their only focus should be on keeping you on your path and providing you with wisdom and support that you need to stay on track. Therefore, you're accountability partner should be someone you look up to and who has accomplished what you are trying to accomplish.

It is strongly recommended that you do not select a family member or a best friend to be you're accountability partner unless they truly demonstrate they will be consistent with their responsibility of challenging, engaging and evoking a sense of accomplishment in you in a neutral and safe environment.

If you do not currently have an Accountability Partner, contact us at br8kfreestrategies@gmail.com. We will connect you to someone in our network that is a great partner and has accomplished what you are trying to get to.

Let's put this all in perspective. My tilting scale is usually weighed heavily on the professional side. I can get so caught up in helping others achieve their goals that I will sacrifice my own personal time. A very good friend who is also my accountability partner helped me to see how my calendar reflected this and challenged me to plan and schedule personal time to do the things that I love. I quickly went to work and found a group on Meetup.com that hosted weekly cycling gatherings at local trails and parks. I now look forward to cycling 10 miles every Saturday morning (which is ideal for my personal energy cycle as I am a morning person!) This group encourages and challenges me each week, so now my cycling time is planned and inserted weekly on my calendar. As a Plan B, I found another cycling group that I can join if there is a Saturday I am unavailable due to events, speaking engagements or other commitments I must attend. You see, as long as I have a plan, I can amend it or change it, but I must start out with one. I also gave my accountability partner permission to ensure I am following the plan I outlined and devoting a minimum of 3 hours per week to focus on hiking or cycling, which in turn helps me to achieve my personal health goals.

Now it's your turn to make a choice!

Are you going to choose to restore balance to your tilting scale regardless of what some may think or say? Will you put together a plan that will focus on YOU? Will you be committed to allocate time to invest in YOU?

Where do you start?

1. Now that you have identified hobbies, passions, things that you like to do, put together your plan.

2. Network with others with similar interests

There are many people who will take their passion, whether personally or professionally and set up a Meetup Groups on www.Meetup.com. Their purpose is to network with others that share their same passion (i.e. cycling, hiking, art, photography, etc.) This is a free networking group! Just a word of caution, if you don't see what you're looking for, try using different search words. Keep in mind you do not want to immediately start a group of your own. You're not looking for additional responsibilities at this point!

3. Set up a weekly schedule, just go and do it!

Now that we've balanced the personal side of the scale, let's begin looking at balancing the professional side of the scale.

STRATEGY 2
THERE'S POWER IN YOUR 'WHY'

What is Your 'Why'?

Before you can say what your 'why' is, let's discuss the definition of what 'why' is and what it is not. 'Why' is defined in the dictionary as (noun) a question concerning the cause or reason for which something is done, achieved. Your 'why' should be defined as the reason that you keep going to achieve your goals even when people, circumstances, or your own mood suggest you should not. Let me share one of my many stories about how my 'why' kept me going.

What I observed in my early childhood formed my behaviors in my adult life as it relates to my commitment in my career. I had the opportunity of watching both my parents be committed to their jobs because they both were performing the work they dreamed about from little children. My father always dreamed of driving trains and my mother dreamed about becoming a nurse. Although they may have experienced challenges, they stayed focused and committed until their dream was realized and they were honored when they both retired from their jobs with over 30 years of stellar performance. For my father, his honor not only came from driving the train, his highest honor came from the countless people he spent equipping and training to do his job during his last 10 years of service.

Because of what I witnessed with my own parents (as you may have), my 'why' became to create a legacy of making a difference by utilizing my talents not just as an employee, but as a business owner. As a result, if any challenges arise in achieving this goal, (and they have and will), my motto is: Anything can be accomplished by NEVER GIVING UP.

In each area of our lives we must have a 'why'. You see, the 'why' is what keeps us going as I said earlier. What keeps you going even when people, circumstances, or your own mood suggests you should not?

_____

_____

_____

_____

_____

Writing down your 'why'

Why should you write down your 'why'? In the year 2000, I wanted to be a Director of Human Resources or have a six-figure salary. By writing down my 'why' I had a goal in front of me that I focused on daily and whenever anything presented itself that went against that goal, it was easy for me to decline. As a result, I was able to achieve not one, but both goals within five years. Actor Jim Carrey often tells the story of his 'why'. As an actor early in his career, he daydreamed of success. One day, he wrote himself a $10 million dollar check and postdated it for 10 years and wrote in the memo "for acting services rendered". He kept that postdated check in his wallet and then in 1994 when his father past away, along with his father he buried the deteriorated check because he accomplished his goal. Jim Carrey was confident his goal would come to pass and believed it so much he put in on paper. There is power in writing down your 'why.'

What is the one thing you want to do more than anything else?

_____

_____

_____

_____

_____

Commitment is defined as doing the things you said you were going to do even after the feeling within you when you said it, has left you. Your 'why' keeps you going even when you don't want to. How many times have you said you were going to do something and at the time you said it you were truly excited and motivated? In your mind nothing or no one could stop you. And then weeks or months later, you allowed someone or a circumstance to prevent you from doing what you said you were going to do.

Not doing what you said you were going to do is probably the main challenge I have found over many years that has prevented hundreds of clients from achieving their 'why.' I remember a client who was full of potential and had all the necessary characteristics for accomplishing great things for both their family and mankind. However, excuses were the common denominator that has her, to this very day, living below her greatness—working a job she dislikes. I remember this client saying, "If I could just move out of this state, I would be able to make more sales to build my business." And she did. She bought a house in another state, only to end up not making any sales and having a longer commute. To our surprise, less than two years after moving, this client, convinced that the new state was the problem, decided to move to yet another state, and yes you have probably guessed what happened, as I write this book, she is still working a job she dislikes. Don't let this happen to you.

It's often said a person can make money or they can make excuses, but they can't make both. Be the person who is committed to their word, NO MATTER WHAT! Do not allow ANY PERSON or "SITUATIONS" to prevent you from doing what you said you were going to do. Period, no excuses, no justifications, no rationalizations. As Nike says, "Just DO IT!" And as Tony Little says, "YOU CAN DO IT!"

I cannot overemphasize this point. When we allow FEAR (False Evidence Appearing Real), people, or situations to disrupt our WHY, we not only cost ourselves and our families the inherent greatness that God has intended for each of us, but more disturbingly, we cost mankind to never see the benefit of our contribution to this world. For example, what if Michael Jackson allowed his family to keep him from performing a solo act? The world would have never known or benefited from his unquestionable entertainment talents. What if Oprah Winfrey used her unfortunate childhood experiences as an excuse to not pursue her dreams? The world would have never known or benefited from all she has accomplished.

The following exercises, when completed, will assist you in determining and remembering your why:

List five individuals you know who are not "world famous", who did not make excuses, and allow people or situations to prevent them from accomplishing their greatness.

_____

_____

_____

_____

_____

Are there any person(s) that you have convinced yourself is keeping you distant from your 'why'? Is that person YOU?

_____

_____

_____

_____

_____

What "situation(s)" are you allowing to dilute your 'why'?

_____

_____

_____

_____

_____

Now, write down your 'why' in the following areas: Why do you want to be an Employee, Self Employed, a Business Owner, or an Investor?

_____

_____

_____

_____

_____

Whether you are an Employee or Entrepreneur, a portion of your 'why' must be greater than you. We will cover this in the next section of leaving your legacy.

STRATEGY #3
Leaving Your Legacy

Defining Legacy

What is a legacy? Legacy is defined as anything handed down from the past, as from an ancestor or predecessor. There are many different types of legacies, but they all fall under two main categories: tangible (money, property, or gifts) and intangible (non-monetary gifts, such as advice or written word—memoirs, books, articles).

What does leaving a legacy mean to you? While on my own Dig In journey, I often asked myself, what am I doing all this for? Why am I putting myself through the pain of being ostracized by friends and family because I am going down a road that is foreign to them? The answers were revealed while taking an internal evaluation of myself. Many people don't like change and I was changing before the eyes my friends and family. You see, I live differently because my focus is on pressing into my relationship with God, so I can have a better life, not only for myself, but for future generations to come. Through my internal evaluation and shift in mindset, wealth both spiritually and naturally has been created for my future generations. To me, this is more valuable than any other legacy I can leave.

What legacy would you like to leave for your future generations?

_____

_____

_____

_____

_____

What do you want to want to pass on? What do you want to be known for?

_____

_____

_____

_____

_____

Always remember, in anything we do, especially changing or creating something new, the hardest thing to do is to begin. Without even realizing it, by picking up this book you have already begun to go about changing your legacy. How? The information you are reading did not come to you by accident. You were created to do good works and those works were prepared in advance for you to do. It was already planned that you would be reading this book, now it is up to you to make the decision to follow your GPS to the next step in your journey, creating your legacy.

Creating Generational Legacy

How would you answer this question: What have you done to share your life experience for future generations?

_____

_____

_____

_____

_____

Whether you are creating a legacy that is tangible or intangible, it starts with building onto who you are and sharing your skills and what is important to you with the rest of the world. For example, I experience a great sense of fulfillment and joy in everything I do! I have the best career; my life's work and my company Br8k Free Strategies allow me to be known as an expert at helping others experience the same. Did I get to this place overnight? No. But now that I am here, I have changed my legacy. How do I share my life experiences for my future generations? I share by writing this book, starting a business, and sharing my experience with the world. You have a story to tell also. Share your life experiences for your coming generations by writing a book.

Ben Franklin said it best, "If you would not be forgotten as soon as you are dead and rotten, either write something worth reading or do things worth the writing." Don't be fooled. Anyone can write a book. If you are an authority on a subject, possess a skill that others wish to learn, have specialized knowledge, solve their problem and write a book. Nothing outlasts your written words.

If you truly have a burning desire to tell your story and create your legacy, send us an email to **br8kfreestrategies@gmail.com,** so you can receive a complimentary 30-minute Best-Seller, Self-Publishing Consultation. Keep reading!

STRATEGY #4

KNOWING YOUR PURPOSE, TALENT & ASSIGNMENT

What is Your Natural Talent?

Your expertise and natural talent is the single most valuable asset you possess. Once you identify and correctly put into action this possession, you will have a life of joy, peace, better health and prosperity. Your expertise is simply the following:

- Experience you have gathered over time in any area of your life along with your natural talents and abilities.
- Valuable 'know how' on at least one topic.

Your natural talent is something we all uniquely have. This is why your unique experiences are worth far more to you than you may realize.

What do you believe are your natural talents and abilities?

_____

_____

_____

_____

_____

What are the experiences that you have gathered over time? What is your expertise or 'know-how' that you know how to do better than most?

_____

_____

_____

_____

_____

Uncovering Your Natural Talent

Why do most people fail to embrace their Natural Talent? One word, conformity.

Here is a story of conformity in action:

A young daughter was watching her mother prepare a large ham for dinner at a family gathering. As she was watching her mother, her mother cut off a pretty large piece of the end of the ham and tossed it aside. The daughter asked her mother why she did this. Her mother proudly said that she wasn't sure, but she learned this from her mother. She went on to say, "If it was good enough for my mother it is good enough for me since my mother was a great cook. "

So the daughter went to her grandmother and asked her why she cut off the end of the ham. Her grandmother proudly said that she learned this from her mother and with the same confidence she said, "If it was good enough for my mother it was good enough for me. My mother was the best cook ever."

So the daughter went to her great grandmother and asked her why she cut off the end of the ham.

Her great grandmother began to laugh and said, "Oh honey, I had to cut off the end of the ham because it would never fit into our little ovens back then."

In this story, it took four generations for one young woman to ask the question, 'why do we do things this way.' How many times have you heard yourself saying those exact words?

Everyone has an untapped reservoir of knowledge, including you. Is this a 'secret'? No. Those who have embraced their Natural Talent have gone on to build successful businesses and are living the life that most just dream about. Remember, this book is about helping you to acquire the skills you need to market the new you!

Take a few minutes to answer these questions.

Where do I naturally excel?

_____

_____

_____

_____

_____

What do I love doing?

_____

_____

_____

_____

_____

What do I want to be known for?

_____

_____

_____

_____

_____

When you discover your unique reservoir of knowledge, your natural talent, what you love to do, you discover your purpose! There is an excitement and you want to share it with the world! You don't look at or worry about anyone else that may have a similar career; you understand that what you have is so unique that people are waiting for you to be the answer to their problem. You understand that there is an Employer looking for someone like you. You start believing there are clients in the world that need your expertise in order to help them accomplish their goals. You walk confidently that there is no one like you! Once this is in place, we now can identify your assignment, which is your Career Path.

Defining Your Career Path

Whether you are or aspire to be an Employee, Self Employed, Business Owner or Investor, when creating and defining your career path, you must be ready to answer "what problem am I here to solve for someone else?" Your success in your career is your ability to stay focused on answering this question while performing assignments & tasks, when interacting with clients (both internal - co-workers, managers, etc. & external- customers, people in the community). We must move away from the WIIFM (what's in it for me) mentality and shift to a career stewardship mentality.

What is career stewardship?

Stewardship is defined as the management or care of something entrusted to one's care. Your career has been entrusted to you, so you must care for every assignment, every interaction and encounter with the utmost care. This is why it is critical to understand the roles you must represent as a career steward. Additionally, it is important to understand how to create a plan when defining your career. In the Human Resources world this is known as a succession plan.

Not by chance but by design, I worked first as an Employee, then Self-Employed, then as a Business

Owner and Investor. I worked for years in each area, but I had extreme F.O.C.U.S. (Follow One Course Until Successful). Each role that is described in the next section can be a stand-alone, meaning you can follow that course until successful and stay in that role or if you are called to do something different you can transition to the next role.

Roles – Employee, Entrepreneur (Self-Employed, Business Owner or Investor)

- Employee - has a job, meaning they work for

someone else.

- Self- Employed - works independently, most often as a Contractor or Consultant, but they own a job
- Business Owner - has employees or contractors working for them; they are a leader and own a system; they are truly their own Boss
- Investor - owns diverse portfolios; always looking for ways for their money work to work for them

Although it is not specified in the four quadrants, I want to note that there are two other professions that are sometimes overlooked but are equally important:

- Foundational Builders - stay at home mom and dads
- Ministry leaders - work & serve the community whether full time or part time

With all the above roles, this is not meant for hobbies or passion. The career path quadrant where someone sits is where their livelihood is dependent on. If they don't work, they do not generate income.

How can you create your career path as an Employee? Very easy, but let me start out by saying that an Employee can have a great career working for someone else. Not everyone is created to own a business. However, it all starts with being able to solve a problem for your employer. The first way to demonstrate this is through your resume. This is the first investment an employee needs to make! Your resume is your manuscript. It should quickly and immediately state your brand - who you are, what your talents are, what you aspire to do and what were the results from the problems you have solved in the past. This is why you must shift your mindset of having friends and family create your resume to making an investment of having one done professionally. A professional resume writer will take great care and pride in showcasing your skills and experience. They will also ensure that you are given every advantage possible by not just focusing on your current status; your resume will be written to focus on where you want to go. Why is this important? Most employers are not just looking to fill a current opening. They are looking at who is going to backfill future open positions, also known as their succession plan. This is how you create your own job. Your resume gets you in the door, then your interview (or as I call it, your conversation) with the hiring manager demonstrates to them that you are the solution to their current problem and you are the answer to their future problems. You go into the conversation with confidence and certainty that you are who they were looking for.

Get rid of any self-limiting beliefs you may have heard or that you told yourself. For example, there have been countless candidates that I have interviewed that walked into the organization without a college degree and even though the job description required the degree, it was rewritten because the candidate had everything we were looking for. I can tell you from personal experience this has happened to me countless times. I had to make a decision that I was going to be a successful employee and it would happen with on-the-job training and mentorship. You see, if I held on to my own personal self-limiting beliefs that I could not grow in my career without a college degree, that belief would have gained strength and restricted my growth. Instead I let go of my self-limiting beliefs and was able to enjoy over 20 years of a fulfilling career in a leadership role in Human Resources.

What self-limiting beliefs, if any, have you allowed to gain power in your life? (education, skills, feedback given by others, etc.)

_____

_____

_____

_____

_____

What are you currently doing that change and influences the lives of the people you come into contact with?

_____

_____

_____

_____

_____

By doing this exercise, your self-limiting beliefs will radically shift as you begin to see how your influence and impact the lives of others around you.

When you have the right resume, can confidently speak to how you are the solution to that employer's problem, consistently demonstrate positive work performance and work towards business strategies and the vision and communicate and work well with all team members gives you the power and authority to create your own career but also your salary. By having this confidence with your employer, you can then build additional income by lending your talents and expertise as a part-time self-employed consultant, which can in turn begin your journey as an Entrepreneur!

STRATEGY #5
FINDING THE RIGHT COACH AND MENTOR

If there was one thing I could teach that would put someone in a position to double their earnings it would be...find the right coach and mentor to guide you. Yes, you need both! Ask any successful CEO, entrepreneur, or manager how they got to the position they are in today, you will most likely hear three names, God and the names of their coach and mentor. When you listen to their story, you hear the same consistent message, being around my mentor helped me on my journey, but working with my coach helped me to do the initial work that was required and often difficult and I was committed, the rest was history.

Understand that Mentoring and Coaching is not the same thing. Mentoring is a power free, two-way mutually beneficial learning situation where the mentor provides advice, shares knowledge and experiences, and teaches using a low pressure, self-discovery approach. People tend to gravitate more quickly to Mentors because of this low pressure approach. Most mentors will not charge for sharing their knowledge. They often open up their office or their home to share their knowledge with you.

A coach will work for you, meaning you are paying them to share their expertise with you and their primary concern is your performance, your ability to change in a specific area(s), and to support you in your goals, vision or career path.

A coach works for you during a specific time frame; however a mentor stays with you for a lifetime. A lifetime? Yes, a lifetime. You become so connected to your mentor that even if you part ways, the teaching, the knowledge and the connection you experience becomes a part of your culture (a way of life) and you duplicate what you've learned with others that cross your path. When people cross my path they understand I have a strong mentorship approach; however when they hire me to be their coach it's a different ball game!

Working with a Mentor is relatively easy. However, working with a coach can be challenging because it requires you to Move out of your Own Way! You must develop the trust, openness and transparency required to trust the process and allow them to speak into your life.

Trusting Your Coach and the Process

Establishing trust may be one of the most difficult things you will have to re-learn. When you grow up you learn not to trust people and it may appear that all anyone cares about is, 'what's in it for me.' When you find the right coach, you must change your mindset if you want to be successful. You may ask, "Why do I need to trust my coach?" Think about it, the best coach will help you with your total life issues and challenges. That means you will need to trust this individual with details that you may have never shared with another soul, so this person must be in a position to help you without any personal gain.

Since you may be working with your coach for some time, rely on your internal sounding alarm to ensure that this person is trustworthy or else you will be wasting your time. Have you ever received a silent, or even sometimes loud alarm, in your head letting you know when someone or something is not right? I remember interviewing for an HR position in the hotel industry. Each time I went for an interview, I felt an unsettling feeling that I could not explain. No matter how many people I spoke with during the interview process, something just didn't feel right. So what did I do? I ignored the signs. It was a great opportunity! So, when the job offer came, I accepted the position and thirty days later I was miserable. After beating myself up and questioning my decision,

I learned to always pay attention to my spirit and always pay attention to the signs. The same rings true when determining if you should trust your mentor. Trust your gut.

Not all coaches will be a good fit for you and your style of learning. I know of instances where clients have left on their own or we discontinued our agreement for no other reason than it was not a good fit. Let's look at it this way. When you start a new job, there is usually a probationary period (this varies in length) which allows time to determine "fit" for you and the employer. Within that probationary period either party, you or the employer, can decide to discontinue any further development of that working relationship after either party discovers the 'fit' is out of alignment. Just like most things in life (finding a job, choosing a car, finding a home, etc.), you may or may not have the "right coach," however, you must make up your mind to keep interviewing and trying out coaches until you find the one that is right for you.

Don't allow naysayers or past experiences to convince you that accomplishing your goals on your own without a coach is a good idea. This mindset will cost you not only money, but more importantly, time that you can **never** replace. Just remember this saying; "There is a price if you do, and a price if you don't. The price you will pay for NOT having a coach will always be greater than trying to accomplish your heart's desire on your own."

Throughout my entire life, the one thing I have noticed consistently is whenever I have followed my mentor and coach; more often than not I was able to achieve my desired results faster, with less stress, and with less money being spent on mistakes. This is true throughout my career and continues in my growing business empire.

Write any mentorship process that you have started and did not complete. Include any reason(s) why?

_____

_____

_____

_____

_____

The Right Mentor and Coach

How do you determine who is the right mentor and coach? Let's look at an analogy. Through your medical insurance plan you select what's called a Primary Care Physician (PCP). You go to your PCP when you need an annual check-up or have unexplained symptoms you cannot diagnose yourself. You rely on your PCP's expertise to ask the right questions, recommend the best specialists to diagnose and treat your symptoms and you trust them to help you feel better. Well, this is exactly what a mentor should do for you. Your mentor freely shares their experience and skills and treats you as a partner versus a student, teacher model. Your mentor will also recognize that they can't and don't know it all and will give you access to their network of specialists/coaches that will aid in helping you perform to meet your goals.

The Right Mentor and Coach should:

1. Not be a friend or family member (remember you need someone that will hold you accountable and tell you what you need to hear, not what you want to hear).

2. Have proven results in the areas you need development.

3. Model and demonstrate the behaviors they expect you to follow (i.e. being on time for appointments, meeting agreed upon deadlines, act with utmost integrity and character, etc.)

4. Not act as your pastor, psychologist, or personal counselor unless they are sufficiently

trained in this area.

5. Keep information confidential and is a positive role model in all areas of their life—especially with their words and actions.

Just as you have expectations of your coach, your coach will have expectations of you. These will include, but are not limited to:

- Acknowledge that what you are doing is not working and you need to change. You must truly believe that you are in need of help or else you will not be open to learn from your mentor.
- Trust your coach in the same manner they trust and believe in your talents and abilities.
- Your commitment to work with your coach. Remember, it took time for you to develop some of the negative behaviors you created, so what would be the reason

you would not commit to correct the
mis-education you have received?

- Maintain professionalism at all times with
  resources and network connections you
  are given access to.

- Always be ready and willing to learn. The
  right coach will expect you to have
  regular, contact with them. It's important
  that you value and appreciate your
  coach's time.

Regardless of how old you are, it is important to
find the right mentor and coach who can continue to
build upon your foundation and help you bring out
what has laid dormant inside of you for many years.
For example, if you are looking to **unleash your
greatness and succeed in your career**, whether you
compete for it (working for someone else) or create it
(working for yourself), having the right strategic
tools and the right mentor will save you time and

energy. If you truly have a burning desire to achieve success, not just a desire (which most people have), but a burning desire, you must be relentless and persistent in finding the right mentor.

Are you willing to make a commitment RIGHT NOW to find the right mentor and coach and follow the guidance they will provide?

If you are ready to be empowered to realize your full potential and ready to unleash your prosperity, email **br8kfreestrategies@gmail.com** and we will connect you with our network of mentors and coaches that are waiting to help you.

SECTION 1 RECAP

When we are determining our career path, often times we want to jump right into the steps of working and building. When we skip the steps of gathering information finding our purpose, our why, our talent, assessment, our support and more importantly maintaining our balance through it all, we do not begin our journey equipped with a solid foundation. This is why our Dig In Process was the start of your journey. If you completed the exercises and journal ed throughout the book, your house is about to be built in warp speed!

Think about, when builders decide to build, whether it's a house or a building, no matter the size of the structure, the foundation is always the longest to put together. They have to make sure that when the land settles, the foundation will stay strong. They have to make sure as they start to build up and out, the foundation will support the weight. Our career deserves the same attention and focus! We want to build up and out on a sturdy foundation.

It started with you making a choice to stay committed with the initial process and making a decision of getting things in order. You were transparent and recognized that in order for things to function properly; you must be a good steward of:

1. Managing Your Time - Balancing your scale personally and professionally.

2. People - Starting with you and then with others

3. Resources - Getting equipped with information from those that have accomplished where you are looking to go

There is one other area that is worth mentioning and that is being a good steward of money. There are so many components to this one area, but we will address it in the Br8k Free section!

Now that your tilting scale is balanced, you've

determined the career path you want to follow as an Employee, now it's time to begin the next leg of your journey!

Let's Go!

SECTION 2

BR8K FREE – THE REVEALING!

After reading this section, you will be able to:

- Br8k Free and Deal with any toxic behaviors and relationships
- Br8k Free and Remove any masks you've been hiding behind
- Acquire the essential skills you need to market the "New You!"

Congratulations!

If you are reading this section, you have uncovered any self-limiting beliefs that were holding you back from Breaking Free to succeed in your career!

You are now armed with your purpose; your 'why', your natural talent, your assignment, and now allow me to act as your Coach to reveal other areas that may be holding you back from being the very best Employee you can be.

In my twenty plus years of working as a Human Resources professional, I have seen countless talented people get fired or even worse, not be considered for a promotion or increase they deserved due to one primary reason... their ATTITUDE!

Your Attitude Determines Your Altitude!

This is why it is critical that before we Br8k Out in our careers that we Br8k Free of any attitudes or behaviors that will hold us back from experiencing our greatest potential in your career. So, I encourage you to not skip this section! I assure you, you won't regret it. Let's Go!

Strategy #1
Removing Your Masks

If you desire to reach your definition of success and purpose, you must reveal and break free from any hidden issues that have been locked away for years that are preventing you from unleashing great power to consistently succeed in your career!

This is generally the place where some say I don't have any issues. What I have found is anyone who claims they don't have any issues are the most dangerous people you can have in your environment.

Everyone has issues. The key is to know which mask is hiding the issues that are blocking your blessings, so you can live the life you were created for.

Defining the Masks

What is a mask? According to the dictionary a mask is a covering for all or part of the face, worn to conceal one's identity; anything that disguises or conceals; disguise; pretense: i.e. his politeness is a mask for his fundamentally malicious personality.

Let's discover together which of the seven (7) masks you have or are currently wearing.

The Mask of Pride: This is the most serious mask of the seven and is the most difficult to remove. This mask is the ultimate source from which the others arise. This mask covers the pain we experience, but fail to talk about (i.e., fear, doubt, abandonment, rejection). This mask also covers up your desire to be more important or attractive than others. When you are wearing this mask you fail to acknowledge the good work of others and you have an excessive love of yourself. It is very important to note that when you have an excessive love of yourself, this often leads to depression.

The Mask of Busyness: This mask covers your actions of appearing lively or "busy" to others, when in fact your activities are having little-to-no-effect on accomplishing your short or long-term goals. For example, most business owners don't realize they are in 'busyness' instead of a business. You will often hear them say, "I don't have any time to do..." This is also true for non-business owners. 'Busyness' is one way of procrastinating and masking fear. I was once an expert at 'busyness' when it came to making a dentist appointment. Every year I knew I should go to the dentist, but I did every activity possible to avoid making that appointment. Why? Simply put, because of fear.

The Mask of Gluttony: This mask hides your over-indulgence and over-consumption of anything to the point of waste.

How many times do you look to food or alcohol for comfort? Have you had excessive unhealthy relationships? Or better yet, how many trips have you taken to the mall for those must-have shoes, outfits or latest electronic gadget, then become frustrated with the amount of debt you have 30 days later?

The Mask of Greed: This mask is put on to defend your actions of disloyalty, deliberate betrayal, manipulation of authority, or trickery for the acquisition of wealth (which is often used for personal gain).

The Mask of Sloth: This mask conceals your failure to utilize the talents and gifts given to fulfill your purpose in life.

The Mask of Wrath: This mask disguises the anger, rage and uncontrolled feelings of hatred you have—either internally or externally.

The Mask of Envy: This mask covers the resentment you have for another person that has something you perceive yourself as lacking and you wish the other person should be deprived of it.

Which mask or masks are you wearing? List all that apply or any other masks (not previously mentioned) that you may be wearing.

_____

_____

_____

_____

_____

There were seasons in my life where I wore four masks at the same time! Talk about a heavy burden! I put on those masks because I was angry. Angry because I was committed to serving the people at my job, yet there was no fulfillment. Angry because I was in a relationship and I was unhappy. So, I put on the mask of wrath. I did not like the anger I was feeling, that is just not my personality. As a result of my being angry, I wanted comfort, so I went shopping for clothes and in the process found great restaurants. While I was shopping and eating, I secured on the mask of gluttony. I wasn't accustomed to all the weight I gained as a result of my comfort food, so I became uncomfortable with how I looked. Now entered the mask of envy. You know what I'm talking about. There are women who can eat whatever they want and still go to the size-6 rack, meanwhile I ate whatever I wanted for four months, and I went from a size 6 to a size 16. I became depressed and frustrated and since I didn't want to focus on the plan I created, I put on the mask of a sloth and did nothing.

It's important to know that the minute you put on your first, second, fourth, or seventh mask, you lose sight of who you are and who you were meant to be. Once you lose sight of who you are, others (your family, friends, significant other, husband, etc.) will define who you should be. Then you will try to be the person you are not. All this leads to frustration, anger and feelings of depression, and the end result is that you become so focused on 'fixing' yourself that you end up 'running.' Running even after you know your purpose. Running even after you have established your goals. Running even after the excitement of creating balance in your life, finding a coach and getting on the right track! This is why we have to sometimes Br8k Free from ourselves to ensure any behaviors or people in or who come into our lives enhance our positive characteristics. In order to Br8k Free we have to start from our beginning and then move forward.

What would you say was the first time you put on your mask and why?

_____

_____

_____

_____

What was the impact of your first decision to put on the mask?

_____

_____

_____

_____

_____

Remember, now that you have identified your beginning, you can choose to move forward! However, understand it is a daily commitment and choice to not go backwards and put the masks on. But sometimes it will happen unexpectedly.

I remember when I was going through a tough time in my life. I was going through a divorce and I was going to a job where I worked with a supervisor that let's just say we didn't see eye to eye. The interesting thing is that I believed no one knew what was going on. To me, it was business as usual without the laughter and smiles I was known to give. Then one day someone on my team came in my office and told me that my team was beginning to resent how I was treating them and that I was different. It was a complete shock to my system. I then realized that I was allowing other people's choices to affect my purpose. The good news is that I remembered what I had previously done during my own Dig In process. I had to pull it out and review my "Why", remember my purpose, and look at where I got off balance. This became my motivation to remove my mask so I could release my blessings.

Remove the Masks, Release Your Blessings

In order to be successful in your career, you must remove your mask to be transparent and open with the individuals you will come in contact with. In order to be open, you must be willing to open up and share. Now I am not saying to tell everyone your personal business, remember you are working in a professional business environment, but what I am saying is to remove your mask and allow people to see the real you - nothing hidden, nothing added, just YOU! Let go of hurts and frustrations - you were looked over for the promotion, things have changed since you got hired, you don't like so and so, and so on and so on...Let It Go! Complaining, putting on masks, and being angry have not and will not change the situation! It's time to make a decision to try something different and that decision is to Be The Real You! Who is that person? The one who was excited in discovering their passions, hobbies, their 'why', their legacy they will leave for loved ones, their purpose and lastly a coach that will help them get to the next level. I'm speaking to that person...The Real You! As your coach I am working with you to get others to see who you really are! Confident, purposeful and focused!

You deserve success, take off your mask and you will receive it!

You deserve to get paid what you are worth, take off your mask and you will receive it!

It's time to decide to Br8k Free of every mask you are wearing that is holding you back. We will remove any other toxic behaviors and relationships; communicate your boundaries, so you can get ready to run your race forward to unleash your greatness. Are you ready to start the process?

Let's Go!

Strategy #2
Dealing with Toxic Behaviors and Relationships

Congratulations! You are no longer hiding behind anger, disappointment, hurt, fear or any other toxic emotions and feelings. The mask is off and is staying off! The new you, is shining bright for the world to see but we must also reveal, unlearn and break any toxic behaviors that were associated with the mask that was being worn for months or years. Where do you start? Let's take a look!

Knowing your worth

If you had to compare yourself to a precious stone, which one would it be?

_____

_____

_____

_____

_____

Years ago, when I asked myself this question, I knew that I would be a diamond. Why? I love diamonds! You can get a variety of different color diamonds, gray, white, blue, yellow, orange, red, green, pink, brown and black. Although I love my chocolate or yellow diamonds, my absolute favorite is the white diamond. Why? When I wear a white diamond it is in its purest state, it remains transparent and colorless, which ties back to my 'Why' and my purpose. In order for me to achieve my mission and vision I need to remain transparent, colorless and always remember not to allow people's emotions, feelings, or behaviors move me from my purest state - Being The Real Me!

Do some research on the precious stone you chose to compare yourself to. How does it tie into the purpose and your 'why' that you identified in Dig In?

_____

_____

_____

_____

_____

_____

When you know you're worth, you will notice that you go to work with a different 'pep in your step'. You will have a strong desire to see the other precious stones that have been in your midst or hidden in your office. You will start to see that although you're worth is invaluable, when you are around other precious stones that look different, when you are knitted together as one the value has increased 100 fold! In other words, although you don't look the same, you have a common goal; to bring your value and contributions to the world so others can value from everyone's beauty, skills, and worth! You can confidently allow your differences to be your strengths! It's also important to note, that when you know you're worth, you will be surprised at how you no longer feel the need to prove anything to people.

No longer a people pleaser

Don't be surprised if people don't jump on the bandwagon of believing you've changed! Remember, just how you've worn a mask, others around you developed their own mask as a defense mechanism against behaviors or actions thrown at them. However, everything you've gone through at this point is not for everyone else, it's for you. Expect the looks and conversations that will stop as you walk in the room. In other words, the only expectation you can have is to expect to hold your head up high, be excited about revealing the Real You and surround yourself with those that will uplift you, support you, encourage you and most importantly, help you to fulfill your purpose, your 'why' that will impact your legacy! Relationships, whether at your job or in your personal life should bring out the best in you. If they don't this could be an indication that you are in or having to deal with a toxic relationship.

If there is anyone or anything in your life that doesn't meet these criteria, it is a must that you re-evaluate their role in your life. I must caution you, before you cut people out of your life it is important that you review strategy 1 and ensure your own masks are off. Often times the way that others have treated you is because you have allowed it. You have accepted them telling you how you should be and what you should be doing. This is why it is important to develop the essential skills necessary to communicate effectively and to have a heart to serve others without compromising who you are.

Remember, you already broke free of being a people pleaser!

STRATEGY #3
COMMUNICATING EFFECTIVELY

"You cannot expect what you don't effectively communicate!" Rhonda Chaplin

---

During a job interview, the candidate must clearly articulate who they are, what skills they bring to the table and the contributions they can make to the organization. Failure to effectively communicate these three points during the initial interview ends the conversation right there. It's no different in personal conversations. Nothing will change, improve or happen when there is a failure to communicate boundaries, expectations, what you will and will not expect.

When we do not communicate effectively:

misunderstandings occur, lack of clarity exists and you are unable to influence matters of life. This is why it is so crucial to understand the fundamentals of communicating effectively because when we embrace this philosophy it branches out in all areas - personally and professionally!

Tips on Communicating Effectively both Personally and Professionally!

- ✓ Communication is the basis of life!
- ✓ The greatest influencer of life is communication!
- ✓ Nothing happens, nothing changes in the absence of clear, concise communication.

Revealing the REAL You!

How do you communicate the Real You? Very simply, always be whom you really are without going back to covering YOURSELF with a mask or settling for less in any relationship. What does that look like?

- ➤ Provide Excellent & Memorable Customer **Serv(e)**-ice at all times! No matter where you are, no matter the response you receive; treat others with respect and the way you want to be treated.

- ➤ Remember you are a precious commodity! Your time, talents, and skills are valuable and should be treated as such by others.

- ➤ Carry yourself as the ultimate professional at all times! In your conversations especially in your interactions with co-workers.

And this only the tip of the iceberg! This is why Br8k Free Strategies offers essential skill development trainings.

Visit www.Br8kFreeStrategies.com for a full detailed listing of our development trainings!

STRATEGY #4
STAYING FREE

Staying on course

Let me warn you to eliminate the distractions that will try to come and take you off course. Trust me they will come. Have you ever been on an airplane that is met with heavier turbulence than expected? Does the pilot turn back? No. The pilot is trained to focus on the instruments in front of them, changes the plan that previously worked, and refocuses on climbing to higher heights to beat the storm that is trying to keep the plane from its final destination. We must do the same thing to remove the distractions that are trying to come against the vision that was set. The distractions are just meant to keep you from your destiny. They are designed to keep you from unleashing your power to succeed. Consequently, since you know the distractions will come, you can focus, train and prepare so you know what to do to beat your storm and to keep the chains that you broke, off!

Keeping the chains off!

Why is staying free the fourth strategy in the Br8k Free System? Very simply, you've done the work, gotten excited about not only discovering your purpose but feeling like you're finally on your way to doing what you've been created to do, worked with your coaches, developed your brand (YOU) Yet, now as you start to share your excitement with others you realize not everyone, including closest family and friends do not share your same excitement. You realize what initially looked so easy for others to do that now you are doing it, you see that it is hard work. That's why strategy #4 is focused on Staying Free! Every employee goes through this stage! However, the employee that stayed the course, kept focus on their vision and wasn't deterred by their thoughts, concerns or what people thought came out a winner! These are the employees that broke their chains and stayed free from what they came out of.

Remember you have already established the importance of having the right people around you. At this stage, this is where you will realize that not missing this step is invaluable. Why? Because you will be surrounded by people that will encourage you, keep you from going back to what is comfortable and help you focus on moving forward daily. Yes, daily! Remember, as an employee you have to choose **every day** to move ahead with the new and make a commitment that you will not go back to anything that you fought, sacrificed, and left behind to Br8k Free and unleash your power to succeed in your career like never before!

Tips to Staying Free!

- Do not isolate! You're not in this by yourself!
  - o Talk to your mentor/coach about what and how you are feeling. Avoid talking about how you feel with anyone who is

not in a position to provide sound advice or they have not been where you are.

- Change what you are listening to!
    o Surround yourself with audios, books, and cds that will encourage, motivate and keep you moving forward!
    o Like the pages on Social Media of motivational speakers you admire! There are many people who I refer to as generals in the business world that regularly provide through their pages encouragement and tips. Just to name a few, some of my favorites include George C. Fraser, Les Brown and Dave Ramsey.
- Learn what you must do to encourage yourself!
    o There will be times on your journey, that you will not have access to your

mentor/coach, social media, etc. So during those times, you have to know how to encourage yourself to keep free!

o Remember your balance scale! What did you determine to be your personal hobbies, interests, or passion? This is the point where you want to do more of your hobby. This will give your mind a break and will remind you of your 'why'. You see, when I break away to go hiking or cycling, I remember that this is part of my 'why'. If I go back to working a job, I will not have the time during the course of the week to enjoy my passions! I will be limited to only enjoying them on the weekends. Going hiking or cycling especially during the week while everyone is working, encourages me to continue to focus on moving forward.

- Keep your vision in front of you
  - When you have a baby, you monitor them 24 x7. If you need to go out you bring the baby with you. You don't leave the baby in the care of just anyone. Just like the newborn baby, you must keep your vision with you at all times. Everywhere you go it goes with you, so you can look at it throughout the day, every chance you get. This will help eliminate those pesky distractions that will try and take you off course!

SECTION 2 RECAP

You have removed your Mask! It is such a pleasure to meet the REAL YOU! You have dealt with any toxic behaviors and relationships that will hinder you from a Br8k Out in your career! Pat yourself on the back!

You have embraced the basics of communicating effectively to all you come into contact with! I'm so happy for you!

Are you excited? I am excited for you!

Now you may feel like you need more development! And that's okay! Remember, Rome wasn't built in a day and certainly wasn't built by one person. We are here to help! You can visit www.RhondaChaplin.com and sign up for a consultation or attend one of our development webinars or events and get additional training. I just don't want you to get stuck in this place because you're foundation is set!

It is time to Unleash Your Greatness so you can soar to new heights! Are you ready? I know you are!

Let's Go!

SECTION 3

BR8K OUT – UNLEASHING YOUR GREATNESS!

After reading this section, you will be able to:

- Get paid what you are worth!

- MOVE UP in Your Current Job! STEP OUT In a Different Job! or TRANSITION to become an Entrepreneur!

- Effectively Develop your Career Brand Strategy

- SOAR in your CAREER!

Congratulations! You did it! Pat yourself on the back! I know there was discomfort involved during the Dig In and Br8k Free process, but the hardest part is over. Now, allow me to Mentor you and assist you in Unleashing Your Greatness, so you can SOAR in the Marketplace! Are you ready? Of course you are! Let's Go!

STRATEGY #1
GETTING PAID WHAT YOU'RE WORTH

Financial Analysis

When was the last time you did a review to see if you are getting paid what you are worth? Annually as the Director of HR, I would ask my Compensation or Recruiting Manager to perform a salary and total compensation analysis of positions to ensure we were competitive in the marketplace. We would submit this information so department heads would budget accordingly. Unfortunately, most candidates would come in for an interview and would either overprice or severely underprice their salary expectations.

But for those of you that are currently working a job, I know what's probably going through your mind, I feel that I am underpaid, how do I get paid what I'm worth when I only receive a 3% annual increase on my job? Very simply! It's not about how you feel, research the current salary for your position in your area and once you have the facts, then Unleash Your Greatness! Work everyday in excellence. Provide the best customer service to customers (both internal - your co-works and external). This is the most important point...Determine what problem are you solving for your department and organization. This is the key to getting paid what you're worth!

First things first!

Take a look at what is going on in your local

market, your industry, and your position. A good starting point is to use (www.Salary.com) to identify the low, middle (median) and high salary for your position (keep in mind the salaries are based on years of position).

What is the middle (median) salary for your position? _____

Are you being paid at least the median salary?

_____

If yes, write down the high salary for your position_____

If no, we have some work to do to Unleash Your Greatness!

Based on your responses above, you will either have to work towards getting paid what you're worth or strive to get towards the higher end of the salary range. Keep your eye on the number you wrote down, either the middle or high salary. That is the number that you will work towards. This number will be your goal whether you STAY at your current job, MOVE UP in your current job, or STEP OUT to a different job.

Notice I did not say to get the salary and march into your boss' office complaining and demanding that you are underpaid. No, you let the new you (your upgraded character and integrity), the work you will perform in excellence with your co-workers who you now see as your team, speak for itself! This is how you will get paid what you're worth when you are working a job. I'll let you in on a little trade secret! Every year, leadership has the ability to provide the top employees in their department with discretionary bonuses or there is an ability to go above and beyond the recommended 2-3% annual increase. Yet these types of bonuses or increases go to those whose job performance (attitude, ability, and work) CONSISTENTLY exceeds the expectation of those in leadership. The funny thing is, you already have in your possession what you need to move your performance from Average to Above

Expectations!

Take a look at your last copy of your performance appraisal. How are your ratings? Do you consistently meet or exceed expectations in all areas?

_____

What are some areas identified where you can excel to get paid what you're worth?

_____

_____

_____

_____

_____

What problem currently exists in your department that you can UNIQUELY SOLVE with your talents and abilities?

_____

_____

_____

_____

_____

Based on your answers above:

Is there an opportunity to solve a problem and STAY or MOVE UP at your current job?

_____

_____

Is it time to STEP OUT to a different job?

_____

Is it time to TRANSITION and solve problems in the marketplace as an ENTREPRENEUR?

_____

_____

Once you establish and are able to demonstrate that you can uniquely solve a problem for the company, you place yourself in a position of power. So, how badly do you want to reap the rewards of your labor at your current or future job? Acquiring a full picture of what you're worth and what the job is worth will arm you with the power you need to negotiate the salary and total compensation package you desire and deserve! Remember, just stating I am not getting paid enough will not get you the money you deserve. Getting emotional will not help your cause, remember you already were able to Br8k Free of that behavior! Facts, concrete examples and information on your value added - meaning problems you solved and the monies you've saved or earned for the company will have you earning a generous salary!

It is also important to note, in order to determine if you are getting paid what you are worth, a financial analysis assessing your current and future state must be performed. When performing a financial analysis, there are many things to review. Current salary, benefits (which are inclusive of 401k, health and life insurance, employee stock options) and any other company perks or discounts. All of this is important when looking to answer the question "am I getting paid what I am worth". There was a time in my career where because I was single, renting, and had no dependents to earn more money would have resulted in me paying more taxes. At the time, I worked with my own Career Advisor and we strategically put a game plan together for me to speak with the Head of HR to ask for Stock Options versus an increase of pay and long term that was a better pay off than receiving a monetary increase. Those stock options enabled me years later to pay a down payment in cash for a house I was purchasing. Understand getting paid what you're worth is not always about the salary or what you see in your paycheck. There are other lucrative benefits that often are missed when the Employee is not trained to look at the total compensation and rewards that is offered at your job.

This is why I do this for clients. I take a look at what is going on in their market because salaries, cost of living and total compensation packages vary widely across the country. I research the range of salaries for their industry and position and am able to help them confidently state with solid facts the range of salaries in their area, the total compensation, the value they will add for the company and their commitment to the company's current and future success. This takes the pressure off the client to do their own independent research and allows them to focus on their development.

Ongoing Development

Ongoing development must be a part of your strategic plan to keep your job and/or to get promoted. Did you know that 80% of your development is your responsibility? Only 20% is your supervisor's. Now, that you know this information, what would be the reason why you would not focus on your development on a daily basis?

Now this is very important. When you are focused on your development, it is critical to focus on the areas of your strengths, which is tied to your purpose that we discussed in Section 1: Dig In! This is very crucial. When we focus on developing our strengths and our passions, we will begin to flourish and excel in areas beyond our imagination! In fact, the job that you may have grown to hate will start to become the work that you love to do. This is why I offer weekly and monthly classes on a variety of topics that aid in Ongoing Career Building Development! When you create, manage and grow Career Strategies, you will have an unstoppable level of positivity, motivation, and engagement that will allow you to reach your fullest potential in everything you do!

While you focus on your strengths, it is important that you have a team of people that will help you manage your areas of opportunity.

Let me give you an example. Early in my career as an Employee, I lived paycheck to paycheck because I spent more than I made. Then one day my boss recommended I sign up for the Employer's 401k retirement plan, which led me to begin taking their online educational courses about Financial

Management. I started to learn the basics of investing, how the stock market worked and how my money would grow, but I certainly was not an expert, nor did I want to become one. This is why I knew it was critical to have a Financial Coach/Advisor to ensure my money was working for me rather than against me.

My Financial Coach/Advisor looked at my 401k plan to ensure I selected the correct funds, looked at my bank savings accounts to see if they yielded the best interest rates, and they helped me to put together a monthly budget to ensure I moved away and never went back to living paycheck to paycheck. This is why I have put together a Development Team to assist clients with reaching their fullest potential in their Career and Finances!

Do you have or want to have the following coaches as part of your Ongoing Development Team?

Resume & Interview Coach - to help you market

your product (YOU) and services (the problem that you will uniquely solve for your Employer) in order to help you get paid exactly what you're worth.

Employment Strategist - helps you to research, develop and maintain your personal and professional employment goals

Financial Coach/Advisor - ensures the money you are getting paid is working for you and not against you

If you are ready to implement strategies to get paid what you're worth and Br8k Out in your career and finances, we have a dynamic team of coaches waiting to help you! Despite what is often stated, Employees can live comfortably and experience Financial Freedom with the right Career Strategies in place!

Now, that you have determined if you're getting paid what you're worth, we now need to address your Career Strategy of whether it's time to MOVE UP in your current job, STEP OUT to a different job or TRANSITION to become an ENTREPRENEUR!

STRATEGY #2
MOVE UP at Your Current Job

Steps to MOVE UP

Often times I have spoken to employees that want to move up in their current job and my first question is always, have you spoken to your supervisor regarding your interest and if they see you being promotable to the next level and often times the answer is "No".

As an employee, if you have the desire to MOVE UP at your current job,

- Step 1: Ensure you are in perfect standing with the company. Meaning you are not on a form of written documentation (write-ups), you do not have a negative performance appraisal on file within the past year, and there is not any other performance or behavioral issues noted on file.

- Step 2: Have a conversation with your supervisor to ensure your desire mirrors with how he/she sees your performance and ability to Move Up. Schedule a meeting and after expressing your interest to growing within the company, ask very specific and direct questions, "Do you see me being promotable to the next level? Why or Why not? If they do, great the next conversation is to determine what the next position is and timing of being promoted. If they don't see you as being promotable, you want to receive specific feedback on what you need to improve on. Get an idea of the how long they view it will take for you to be on track to be considered for the next available open position

- Step 3: Work with someone who can assist you with putting together a game plan to strategically work on the areas pointed out by your supervisor

- Step 4: Follow up! Check in regularly with your supervisor to get feedback on your performance and the areas discussed for needed improvement. Your focus is not on discussing the promotion, it's to get feedback on how you are doing since the last meeting.

If you have a strong desire to MOVE UP, you will need to take complete ownership of your development. Keep in mind, 80% of your development is your responsibility, 20% is your supervisors. If you want to MOVE UP, you will need to take control and based on the feedback you receive, that is the development you want to focus on. For example, early on in my career, I expressed an interest of growing into management. My manager at the time stated I would need to improve in my communication. She stated that I have great ideas that I would share in her office, however, she wanted me to speak up in meetings instead of staying quiet. Well, needless to say, my first response was 'forget it'! My shyness and also being a strong introvert who processes information before speaking led me to shrink back and stay quiet in public forums. After having my temper tantrum, I had to ask myself the question, "How bad do I want to MOVE UP" and I wanted it badly! So, I signed up for Toastmasters and learned the art of public speaking and how to process information quickly in order to effectively communicate my thoughts. I made monetary investments to attend workshops and training classes to work on every area of opportunity that was pointed out by my supervisor. I practiced every chance I had to share my ideas without worrying about making a mistake or being wrong. Well, my supervisor took notice of my receiving her feedback and improving in this area. She did not know nor did she need to know what I was doing in order to improve in my communication. All she needed to know and see was that I was working on the areas she noted and as a result six months after the conversation, I was able to MOVE UP into my first managerial role! So now I ask you:

How bad do you want to MOVE UP in your current job?

_____

_____

_____

Are you willing to do what it takes to get the development you need to MOVE UP?

_____

_____

_____

Once you have the initial conversation expressing your interest of growing with the company, it is not necessary to repeat your desire. In companies that have a culture of internal promotions, there are quarterly discussions known as succession planning meetings that are held with Department Heads and HR to discuss who's promotable now, in 6 months or 12 months. It is also noted the development that needs to happen in order for that employee identified to grow and the manager will submit their plan to the HR Manager. So you see, once you or your manager expresses interests in your growth with the company, you no longer have to chase them down. Allow the HR department to do that for you, all you have to do is work on the areas identified to get you to your next level.

Your Career Game Plan

Understand that when you have a desire to MOVE UP, there must be a commitment, focus and investments made on your part in order to achieve your goal. Remember what we said earlier in the Br8k Free Section "You're attitude determines you're altitude". If you have the right attitude, you will notice that the investments you make will pay off greatly. You see the investments I made for the workshops and training classes didn't just benefit me for that job, it benefited me for my entire career from Manager to Director of HR to running my own business. I want you to also look at from that perspective. You're building your career. Your commitment, focus and investments are to help you for the duration of your entire work history. This is why just for reading this book, I have for you a Personal Career Game Plan and access to my essential skills development training. All you have to do is send an email to br8kfreestrategies@gmail.com and put Career Game Plan in the subject line and we'll get you on the road to MOVE UP at your current job!

Now, as with anything in life, there are no guarantees. You may do the 80% that is required for you to focus on your ongoing development.

However, business or leadership may change, the company may decide to go in a different direction, or the duration of time to get promoted may shift. When these things happen, although you may have the best intentions of STAYING with your current job, you may have to shift to the idea of taking all that you have learned, your experiences, and your knowledge to STEP OUT to a different job! Are you ready to explore this thought? I know you are! Let's Go!

STRATEGY #3
STEP OUT to a Different Job

You have accessed that it is or it may be time to take a leap and STEP OUT to a different job! How exciting! You have an opportunity to get aligned with a company that you can provide excellent Serv(e)-ice, get paid what you deserve, and be able to grow and SOAR! In order to find the right opportunity, we need to get your brand message into the hands of the decision makers of the companies you have researched and want to work for. How do we do this? First identify the company's in your field that you want to work for. Do your homework! Start out by going directly to the company website to find out more about them (this will aid you during the interview when you're asked the question what do you know about the company). Secondly, utilize sites like Glass Door, LinkedIn, CareerBuilder and find out what others are saying about the company!

After you've narrowed down a selection of company's, let's shift our focus on Marketing You, the Employee, and the Service you will uniquely provide. This starts with Your Resume.

Over my 20 years of reviewing resumes, I can always tell when a candidate has made the decision to have a DIY Resume. You know what I mean! A Do It Yourself Resume and if I can be candid, it shows! A DIY resume does not tell a candidate's story. It barely speaks of key accomplishments, contributions made to their workplace and results brought to the company. Nor is the resume tailored to the organization that they are looking to work. It is always amazing to me how candidates would not have these key points on their resume and they were unable to speak to these points during the interview. Let's be real. HR and the hiring managers are looking for you to answer 3 main questions:

- How will you solve the problem they currently have
- Will you be able to adapt to the culture of the organization and the team
- What significant contributions will you bring to the table and will you be able to grow to the next level. Meaning, are you promotable to the next level.

Answer these 3 questions on your resume and during the interview and you have the power to get paid what you are worth. But so many times, we have this DIY mentality instead of making an investment to have a resume professionally done by someone who is experienced, not as a writer, but as a seasoned HR Business Professional.

Here is an example:

Two years ago, I received a UPS package from a candidate interested in an opportunity within the IT department. In the position requirements it stated we were looking for innovative candidates who had a desire to excel in the world of IT. Along with his professionally done resume, the candidate took an old iPhone, embedded his cover letter into the screen and stated why he was the best candidate for the job.

Now what he did may seem basic in writing, but I want you to understand that the candidate took the time to understand the need of the company (innovation), made an investment to tailor his resume to his accomplishments, results and his desire to get into management (establishing his growth strategy) and most importantly, he set himself apart from every candidate that just emails or responds to the posting online. This candidate was immediately brought in for an interview and his confidence, conversation and presentation mirrored what was presented on his resume. Needless to say, after 2 rounds of interviewing, he got the job!

How about you? If a former boss or former co-worker recommended you for a position, do you have a well written resume available to send them? Would you be able to clearly, confidently and concisely answer the three questions mentioned earlier?

_____

_____

_____

_____

_____

Just as critical as it is to have a resume that will speak to who you are and the talents you will bring to the organization, you will need to strongly communicate what is represented on your resume.

128

Communicating Your Message

It is important to note that the resume will only bring you in the door, your communication, presentation and message is what will allow you to enter the door and soar! The easiest way to think of the interview is as a conversation. Look at it that you are going in armed, equipped and confident that this job and opportunity is yours! They just don't know it yet. What I am saying is if you see it as a conversation it will reduce the nervousness that you may have. This is where having an interview coach will help you prepare your responses in a SMART way. SMART is an acronym that is used by many employers to ensure they are receiving specific responses to their questions during the interview. The SMART acronym stands for:

- Specific - what was done?
- Measurable - did the task outcome meet expectations?

- Achievable - how did you do it?

- Relevant - what was the impact? how was the task in alignment with department goals

- Time Oriented - did you meet the deadline? How long did it take?

Remember, in addition to listening to how your communicating your message with your words and responses, the other person in the conversation is watching out for how you communicate via listening, your non-verbals and your presentation (how you look). This is what I look for and listen out for with my clients. I say all the time, "It's not what you say, but how you say it and how you look while you're saying it!"

Presentation, both verbal and non-verbal is so critical to finding the job, getting the job, and keeping the job! Now that we have focused on you, we now need to look at where we will Network in order to get your message in front of the right people.

Networking

Strategic marketing is critical if you want to land the job at the employer of your dreams. You have to go and be where they are. I remember when I realized the next step in my career in Human Resources was to gain experience in Employee Relations. Back then we didn't rely on computers; we had the NY Times Classified section to find out about job postings. One Sunday, I saw a company had a posting for an Employee Relations Manager. I updated my resume so it reflected the position and faxed it over. I then found out there was a career fair and they were one of the companies listed to be in attendance. Needless to say, I used one of my vacation days to ensure I would be in attendance at the career fair. Once there, I walked up to the table, introduced myself, asked the representative who turned out to be the Sr. Director of HR what qualifications they were looking for in the Employee Relations Manager and after he responded, I confidently stated "I am the person you have been looking for to fill this position. Please review my resume and I will make myself available to interview for this great position at your earliest convenience". The next day I received a call to come in and within two weeks I was offered the job. This technique has not only served me, but several clients that I recommended the same approach. In this day and age, you have to utilize both offline and online techniques to Br8k Out from the pack!

There are great resources to ensure YOU are Marketed professionally online. The number one resource is Linked In! Everyone should have a professional profile created that clearly outlines your Brand message. I believe so strongly in this because Recruiters and Executives go to LinkedIn as a top resource when looking for top talent or experts to solve a problem in their organization. If you do not have a professionally done profile on Linked In this is a MUST, so contact me today and I will connect you with one of our Resume and Interview Coaches that will help you put your profile together!

As you STEP OUT to Market You, Communicate your message and Network to find a different job, do not get discouraged when you hear the word NO. NO just is another acronym for **N**ext **O**pportunity. Keeping going until you get YOUR YES! If you feel stuck, it may be an opportunity to consider investing in a Resume and Interview Skill Coach to help you market your product (YOU) and your services (the problem that you will uniquely solve for your Employer), in order to help you get where you are looking to go!

It is important to note, that sometimes when we step out to a different job it may not be to another employer. There may be some of you reading this book that will step out to a different job of full time ministry or a full time foundation builder (a stay at home mom or dad). For these two also very important jobs, the steps really remain the same. You may not need a paper resume, however, your skills and abilities need to remain at the forefront of your heart. Although your pay will come from other sources, you impact people and our future generation so greatly that you will need to provide excellent Serv(e)-ice, determine how you will solve a problem they currently have, bring significant contributions to the table and be able to grow and SOAR in your roles in full time ministry or foundation builder!

Now let's turn our attention to the Employee that has made the decision to begin their TRANSITION from EMPLOYEE TO ENTREPRENEUR!

STRATEGY #4

TRANSITION TO BECOME AN ENTREPRENEUR

Very much like an Employee, being an Entrepreneur, a Business Owner, starts with answering the same question: What unique products and services will you provide to solve a problem in the marketplace which will in turn allow you to get paid exactly what you're worth. Without answering this question, you will develop a hobby and not a business. This is why 8 out of 10 entrepreneurs who start a business fail within the first 18 months. That's 80% who lose their financial investment. That's 80% who end up going back to working a job. That's 80% that did not take the time to figure out their true unique value they bring to the table that is different than others in the marketplace.

But get excited! You did the work already! If you completed your Dig In Strategies work in Section 1, you have your purpose (your unique value), so we can now turn our attention to developing your vision and determining what your products and services should be.

As exhilarating as it is to envision your dreams coming alive, it is imperative that you understand that although I am providing this information in this book, I strongly recommend that you acquire a New Business Development Coach to help you design your business model strategies. It will be more cost effective in your time and for your finances to get a coach to help you Br8k Out in Your New Business Development Model! Are you ready? Let's Go!

New Business Development

Did you know that the first step to transitioning to an Entrepreneur is to begin with establishing your vision statement? Since you already have your 'why' and your purpose, you now need to establish your vision statement as this will clearly and concisely communicate your business' overall goals. It will also define the core ideals as your business begins to take shape and direction.

Your vision statement will also serve as a tool for all decisions made in your company. This statement can be as simple as a single sentence or a short paragraph.

Don't worry about making a complete sentence. In a few words, what do you see your business accomplishing? What is the goal or end result for your client? What problem are you looking to uniquely solve?

_____

_____

_____

_____

_____

Jot down a minimum of 6 words describing the following. What are your values? What is important to you?

_____

_____

_____

_____

_____

After I completed these exercises with my coach, I was able to come up with my vision of my business *"Helping Employees and Entrepreneurs Realize their Full Potential to Unleash their Greatness in the Marketplace."* I accomplish this by never deviating from my beliefs and values of being Resourceful, Collaborative, Convicted, and Operating with Integrity!

Hopefully, you have jotted down a few words or sentences! Now is a great time to jump start your TRANSITION! Remember, I've been where you are right now! Go to www.RhondaChaplin.com and schedule a 30-Minute Complimentary Coaching Session.

Now that you have your vision, the next step is to identify what products and services you will offer in the marketplace. Can you feel your greatness being unleashed? Don't forget, this is the fun and exciting part of the journey! You are doing all of this because you have a solution to someone else's problem! This is your purpose and it is your time. Let's take a look at what you will bring to the marketplace!

Identify Your Products and Services

What are some things that you do on a regular basis that you enjoy and people always recommend you to others?

_____

_____

_____

_____

_____

What makes the things that you do or offer unique from anyone else? (If you're not sure, ask for feedback from others that seek you out for your products or services)

_____

_____

_____

_____

_____

What are some things that you see in the marketplace that aggravates you? (i.e. declining Customer Service, lack of natural/healthy food options, etc.)

_____

_____

_____

_____

_____

Often times we start out thinking that the only products and services we can offer are things we have spent years doing. What I have found is that we have an opportunity to unleash the greatness in us that was hiding. These things are found in the very area that angers us! What we don't realize is sometimes what angers or vexes us is the very thing we were created to fix and that becomes the leading product and service that we can bring to the marketplace. For example, with the ever growing field of technology, communication, presentation and engagement has become a long lost area of focus between generations. As a strong communicator, this became an area that would annoy me. In my annoyance, I created a service that solved a problem to bridge the communication gap between the different generations working together within their places of work and this became the catalyst for me to engage in training workshops with Employees at many different companies.

Additionally, I ensured I was able to get feedback from customers. I was able to find out if they see a need for a variety of products and services that I now offer to the marketplace. I would encourage you to do the same. Get feedback from clients, co-workers and go to different networking events. This will enable you as a Business Owner to offer the right services, at the right time, and be in a position to have the right team around you!

Identifying Your Team

Going from being a Good to a Great Entrepreneur starts with having the right people around you.

You will need a great team that will push you beyond your limits. A great team is like a 5 course meal. From the beginning to the end, it will feed you all the necessary ingredients to keep you nourished, full and feeling complete. Nothing is left out with every course that is served! Whereas, a good team is like a piece of chocolate cake; it will temporarily satisfy your current needs of having something sweet, but in the long run it isn't long lasting. It doesn't satisfy all of the nutritional needs that your body needs to sustain itself.

Building a New Business is not the time to incorporate a DIY (Do It Yourself) Mindset! You will need a great team to help you build your business infrastructure, Business Entity Formation, Business Branding, establishing your Business Infrastructure, and much more. Take it from someone who tried to do it all herself, it cost me a lot of time, a lot of money and did I mention a lot of time! I ended staying as an Employee longer than I had to because I did not want to make the investment of having a great team of experts to do what they do which allowed me to spend my time doing what I love and what I am great at, building careers!

Understand that in the Br8k Out system we are talking about five areas that will be considered your core team. They are:

- People

- Marketing
- Sales & Fulfillment
- Finance & Accounting
- Technology

It is critical to get a system around your business from the very beginning. Because I am committed to seeing you soar, I am putting you in a position to 'borrow' my team until your business is up and running and you have networked and have all the right people positioned around you!

Great news! You have enough information and you've done enough DIY work by completing the exercises in this book! Now, you're ready for a New Business Development Coach to help you pull this all together so you can Unleash Your Greatness as an Entrepreneur in the Marketplace! If you go to www.Br8kFreeStrategies.com, you will find a list of events, online classes and coaching options that assist you in bringing life to your new baby! Yes, your business will become your baby that you will have the pleasure of creating, managing, nurturing and watching it grow!

You have been on quite a journey while reading this book! Think about it. Your purpose, your 'why' and your natural talent were UNCOVERED. The REAL YOU has been REVEALED. You have UNLEASHED YOUR GREATNESS in your current or future job or as an entrepreneur. So, what's left for you to do! Well, that's easy to answer! It's time to SOAR!

Let's Go!

STRATEGY #5
SOAR!

Let's GO!

" When you create, manage, and grow Career Strategies, you have an unstoppable level of positivity, motivation, and engagement that will allow you to reach your fullest potential in everything you do!" *Rhonda Chaplin*

According to Merriam-Webster, the definition of SOAR is to fly or rise high in the air, to increase rapidly above the usual level. To maintain height in the air without flapping wings or using engine power.

In other words to SOAR means more than just to fly; it means to rise swiftly, to feel the wind slipping below you as you ride it higher, higher, higher. Flying is just moving through the air. SOARING, suggest exhilaration, even joy!" (Vocabulary.com)

You are ready to SOAR! You can rise swiftly because you are armed with your Career Strategy. Your Career Strategy indicates if you are going to MOVE UP in your current job, STEP OUT to a different job or TRANSITION to become an Entrepreneur. As you work with your coach and get in position you will ride higher, higher, and higher! You will be unstoppable in your job or in your business!

Here are some key Strategy Reminders as you take off and SOAR:

- Remain balanced! Your balance is the key to your success. Do not become so busy that you neglect being balance in personal and work.
- Communicate with your coach! Your coach has a vested interest in seeing you be successful. They are there to help you through the good, the bad and the great!

While you are soaring and gliding through your journey, do not pick up the DIY mentality. Talk things through with your coach.

- Stay on course! Walk with your career strategy everywhere you go! Have it in your car, your purse, your wallet. Keep it in front of you, so no matter what you hear or see, nothing will move you out of path you worked so hard to uncover and reveal!

- Always be ready! Whether you are running errands, going to an event, or just hanging out with friends and family, always be armed and ready to show the marketplace your greatness! This ranges from your appearance (always dress to impress) to having your resume or business cards handy. You never know whom you will meet.

- Soar and Rise Swiftly! Be unstoppable.
  Provide excellent serv(e)-ice to everyone you
  come in contact with.

- Every day make a conscious decision to
  Unleash Your Greatness!

Remember, you are the unique solution to a problem in the marketplace. You are great and awesome and others need what you have. They are waiting for you! This is your time to bring your greatness to the Marketplace and SOAR!

LET'S GO!

FINAL NOTE

It has been an honor and a pleasure to join you on your journey! But don't worry! I am so glad to report that the journey does not end here. Ongoing development will be key to keep soaring higher and higher. Stay connected through Facebook, my website, events, online classes and YouTube channel. I am committed to providing you ongoing strategic resources, materials, and information so you can continuously SOAR and SUCCEED in your career like never before!

Additional Resources:

- ✓ Visit the Employee Suite or Entrepreneur Suite at www.RhondaChaplin.com for more information on my Training, Coaching and Development Programs.

- ✓ Connect with me on our Social Media Pages:
  - Twitter and Persicope (@RhondaChaplin)
  - Facebook (br8kfreestrategies)

ABOUT THE AUTHOR

Rhonda is a highly sought after communication and facilitation expert who delivers engaging learning experiences. She has over 20 years of broad experience in corporate and not-for-profit agencies as a Human Resources Professional. As the former Director of HR for a billion dollar organization, Rhonda was responsible for a team of HR specialists that provided services to more than 30,000 employees in the US and Canada.

Rhonda founded Br8k Free Strategies, LLC and Free Day Strategies, LLC. to empower her clients to unleash their greatness in their career. Through her development sessions, conferences and books, Rhonda inspires clients and colleagues with a deep understanding of their individual situations and provides strategies to realize their career goals.

Br8k Free Strategies, LLC
www.br8kfreestrategies.com